D0987954

PET

# FIVE
# FINGER-PIGLETS

*Also published by Macmillan*

ONE OF YOUR LEGS IS BOTH THE SAME
Poems by Adrian Henri, Terry Jones,
Michael Rosen, Colin McNaughton
and Kit Wright

ANOTHER DAY ON YOUR FOOT AND
I WOULD HAVE DIED
Poems by John Agard, Wendy Cope,
Roger McGough, Adrian Mitchell
and Brian Patten

WE COULDN'T PROVIDE FISH THUMBS
Poems by James Berry, Grace Nichols,
Judith Nicholls, Vernon Scannell
and Matthew Sweeney

# Five Finger-Piglets

*Poems by*
**Carol Ann Duffy**
**Jackie Kay**
**Roger McGough**
**Gareth Owen**
**Brian Patten**

*Illustrated by* **Peter Bailey**

MACMILLAN CHILDREN'S BOOKS

First published 1999 by
Macmillan Children's Books
a division of Macmillan Publishers Ltd
25 Eccleston Place London SW1W 9NF
and Basingstoke

Associated companies throughout the world

ISBN 0 333 71263 3

This collection copyright © 1999 Macmillan Children's Books
Poems in this selection © 1999 Carol Ann Duffy, Jackie Kay, Roger McGough,
Gareth Owen, Brian Patten.
Illustrations copyright © Peter Bailey 1999

Selection edited by Gaby Morgan.

The moral right of the authors has been asserted.

1   3   5   7   9   8   6   4   2

A CIP catalogue record for this book is available from the British Library.

Typeset by Macmillan Children's Books
Printed by Mackays of Chatham PLC, Kent

# Contents

# Moon

'The moon is thousands of miles away,'
My Uncle Trevor said.
Why can't he see
It's caught in a tree
Above our onion bed?

Gareth Owen

# The Kleptomaniac

Beware the Kleptomaniac
Who knows not wrong from right
He'll wait until you turn your back
Then steal everything in sight:

The nose from a snowman
(Be it carrot or coal)

The stick from a blindman
From the beggar his bowl

The smoke from a chimney
The leaves from a tree

A kitten's miaow
(Pretty mean you'll agree)

He'll pinch a used teabag
From out of the pot

A field of potatoes
And scoff the whole lot

(Is baby still there,
Asleep in its cot?)

He'll rob the baton
From a conductor on stage

All the books from the library
Page by page

He'll snaffle your shadow
As you bask in the sun

Pilfer the currants
From out of your bun

He'll lift the wind
Right out of your sails

Hold your hand
And make off with your nails

When he's around
Things just disappear

F nnily eno gh I th nk
Th re's one ar und h re!

Roger McGough

# The Bogeyman at Number Twelve

The man in the darkness on the top stair
Is always pretending not to be there

Deep in the dark on the very top stair.

The man in the darkness on the top stair
Whispers so quietly only I hear

His voice in the darkness on the top stair.

And I'm never certain that it's him there,
For the man in the dark on the top stair

Is shadowy faint and thin as the air.

And when the dawn creeps up to the top stair,
I can never work out exactly where

He stood in the darkness on the top stair.

He can vanish like stars, like mist into air,
And leave only a black cat licking its fur,

Curled up in the sunlight on the top stair.

Brian Patten

# Brendon Gallacher
## (for my brother, Maxie)

He was seven and I was six, my Brendon Gallacher.
He was Irish and I was Scottish, my Brendon Gallacher.
His father was in prison; he was a cat burglar.
My father was a communist party full-time worker.
He had six brothers and I had one, my Brendon Gallacher.

He would hold my hand and take me by the river
Where we'd talk all about his family being poor.
He'd get his mum out of Glasgow when he got older.
A wee holiday someplace nice. Some place far.
I'd tell my mum about my Brendon Gallacher

How his mum drank and his daddy was a cat burglar.
And she'd say, 'why not have him round to dinner?'
No, no, I'd say, he's got big holes in his trousers.
I like meeting him by the burn in the open air.
Then one day after we'd been friends two years,

One day when it was pouring and I was indoors,
My mum says to me, 'I was talking to Mrs Moir
Who lives next door to your Brendon Gallacher
Didn't you say his address was 24 Novar?
She says there are no Gallachers at 24 Novar

There never have been any Gallachers next door.'
And he died then, my Brendon Gallacher,
Flat out on my bedroom floor, his spiky hair,
His impish grin, his funny flapping ear.
Oh Brendon, Oh my Brendon Gallacher.

Jackie Kay

# Sloppy Ticks

Why are kisses crosses
When you put them on a letter?
Big, juicy, sloppy ticks
Would be so much better.

Roger McGough

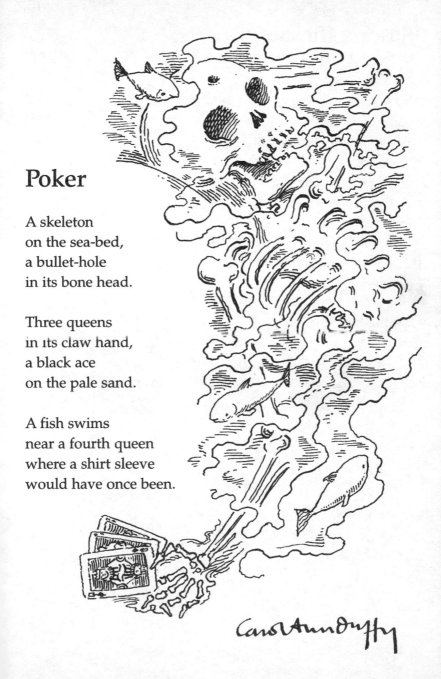

# Poker

A skeleton
on the sea-bed,
a bullet-hole
in its bone head.

Three queens
in its claw hand,
a black ace
on the pale sand.

A fish swims
near a fourth queen
where a shirt sleeve
would have once been.

Carol Ann Duffy

# Playing the Baby
# at Number Twenty-Five

When I want to play music loud
People complain:
'Turn that !@#*! music down!'
It's a pain.
It gets me down because

When the woman next door
Wants to play her baby loud,
If I shout, 'Turn that baby down!'
Guess what?

Nothing happens.

*Brian Patten*

# Our School

I go to Weld Park Primary,
It's near the Underpass
And five blocks past the Cemetery
And two roads past the Gas
Works with the big tower that smells so bad
       me and me mates put our hankies over our
            faces and pretend we're being attacked
                  by poisoned gas . . . and that.

There's this playground with lines for rounders,
And cricket stumps chalked on the wall,
And kids with their coats for goalposts
Booting a tennis ball
Around all over the place and shoutin' and arguin'
       about offside and they always kick it over
           the garden wall next door and she
               goes potty and tells our head teacher
               and he gets right ratty with
                  everybody and stops us playin'
                  football . . .
                     . . . and everything.

We have this rule at our school
You've to wait till the whistle blows
And you can't go in till you hear it
Not even if it snows.

And your wellies get filled with water and your socks
go all soggy and start slipping down your legs
and your hands get so cold they go all
crumpled and you can't undo
the buttons of your mac when
you do get inside . . .
. . . it's true.

The best thing is our classroom.
When it's fine you can see right far,
Past the Catholic Cathedral
Right to the Morris Car
Works where me dad works as a fitter and sets off
right early every morning in these overalls
with his snap in this sandwich box and
a flask of tea and always moanin'
about the money . . . honest.

In Hall we pray for brotherly love
And sing hymns that are ever so long
And the Head shouts at Linda Nutter
Who's always doing wrong.
She can't keep out of trouble because
she's always talkin'
she can't stop our teacher says she
must have been injected with
a gramophone needle she talks
so much and
that made me laugh once
not any more though I've heard it
too often . . . teachers!

Loving your enemy sounds all right
Until you open your eyes
And you're standing next to Nolan
Who's always telling lies
About me and getting me into trouble and about
　　　three times a week I fight him after school
　　　　　it's like a habit I've got
　　　　　　　but I can't love him even though
　　　　　　　　　I screw my eyes up real hard and try like
　　　　　　　　　　mad, but if it wasn't him it
　　　　　　　　　　　would be somebody else
　　　　　　　　　　　I mean
　　　　　　　　　　　　　you've got to have enemies . . .
　　　　　　　　　　　　　　　. . . haven't you?


We sing 'O to be a pilgrim'
And think about God and heaven
And then we're told the football team lost
By thirteen goals to seven
But that's not bad because St Xavier's don't half have
　　　big lads in their team and last time we played
　　　　　they beat us eighteen one and this time
　　　　　　　we got seven goals . . .
　　　　　　　　　. . . didn't we?


Then we have our lessons,
We have Science and English and Maths,
Except on Wednesday morning
When our class goes to the baths

And it's not half cold and Peter Bradberry's
fingers went all wrinkled and blue last week
                and I said, 'You're goin' to die, man'
                        but he pushed me under the water and I had to
                                hold my breath for fifteen minutes.
                                        But he's still alive though . . .
                                                . . . he is.

Friday's my favourite day though,
We have Art all afternoon
And I never care what happens
Cos I know it's home-time soon
And I'm free for two whole days but I think
        sometimes it wouldn't be half so good
                having this weekend if we didn't have five
                        days
                                of
                                        school
                                                in
                                                        between –

Would it?

*Gareth Owen*

# Summer Romance

I was best friends with Sabah
the whole long summer;
I admired her handwriting,
the way she smiled into
the summer evening,
her voice, melted butter.
The way her chin shone
under a buttercup.
Everyone let Sabah
go first in a long
hot summer queue.
The way she always looked
fancy, the way
she said 'Fandango',
and plucked her banjo;
her big purple bangle
banged at her wrist;
her face lit by the angle
poise lamp in her room,
her hair all a tangle,
damp from the summer heat,
Sabah's eyes sparkled all summer.

But when the summer was gone
and the winter came,
in walked Big Heather Murphy.
Sabah turned her lovely head
towards her. I nearly died.
Summer holidays burn with lies.

*John Tiernan*

# Bun Fight

The buns are having a fight
There are currants on the floor
The custards egg them on
'More,' they cry, 'more.'

The doughnuts form a ring
'Ding, ding!' and the seconds are out
An eccles cake is taking bets
As to who will win the bout.

The referee is a muffin
The time-keeper is a scone
There are five rounds still to go
And the custards egg them on.

The chelsea bun is tiring
And hoping for a draw
When the bath bun throws an uppercut
That brings him to the floor.

The muffin slowly counts him out
And the bath bun's arm is raised
While through the window, passers-by
Look into the cake-shop, amazed.

Roger McGough

# A Bird, Dropping

There's no stopping
A bird dropping.

# Lies

I like to go out for the day and tell lies.
The day should be overcast
with a kind of purple, electric edge to the clouds;
and not too hot or cold,
but cool. I turn up the collar of my coat
and narrow my eyes.

I meet someone –
a kid from school perhaps –
and give him five.
Then I start to lie
as we walk along Tennyson Drive kicking a can.
He listens hard,
his split strawberry mouth moist and mute,
my weasel words
sparking the little lights in his spectacles.
At the corner of Coleridge Place
I watch him run,
thrilled, fast, chasing his breath,
home to his mum.

Bus stops I like,
with long, bored, footsore, moaning queues.
I lie to them
in my shrill, confident voice,
till the number 8 or 11 takes them away
and I stand and stare at the bend in Longfellow Road,
alone in the day.

At the end of the darkening afternoon
I head for home,
watching the lights come on in truthful rooms,
where mothers come and go
with plates of cakes,
and TV sets shuffle their bright cartoons.
Then I knock on the door of 21 Wordsworth Way,
and while I wait
I watch a spaceship zoom away overhead
and see the faint half-smile of the distant moon.
They let me in.
And who, they want to know, do I think I am?
Exactly where have I been? With whom? And why?
The thing with me –
I like to come home after a long day out
and lie.

Carol Ann Duffy

# Life as a Sheep

Sometimes
Oi stands
Sometimes
Oi sits
Then
Stands again
Then
Sits
For a bit.

Sometimes
Oi wanders
Sometimes
Oi stays
Sometimes
Oi chews
Sometimes
Oi strays.

Sometimes
Oi coughs
Sometimes
Oi don't
Sometimes
Oi bleats
Sometimes
Oi won't.
Sometimes
Oi watch

The human race
Or
Smiles to meself
Or
Stares into space.

And when
Oi's happy
Oi'd dance and sing
But Oi
don't have the knack
To do
Such a thing.

At night
Oi lays
By the old church steeple
And
Falls asleep
By counting people.

*Gareth Owen*

# Pomegranate
## (for Chorlton Park School)

See, if it hadnie been for Persephone,
you'd have thought someone
was having you on
when you first clapped eyes on:
snow, a bald tree, yellow grass,
or happened to pass
a snowman in a field of frost,
or an icicle hanging from a sash-
windie, or bare roses, lashing sleet or slush.

You'd have never failed an exam,
because you simply wouldnie have gone
to school. You'd have had summer holidays
– a summer holiday symphony always –
if Persephone had clocked the Golden Rule,
and kept her beautiful lips sealed;
if she had not sucked those six small reds,
down in the deep dark world of the dead,
where every tree had lost its big head.

Next time someone offers you a wee bite of fruit –
think seriously for a second, then scoot.

_Jackie Kay_

# Can We Have Our Ball Back, *Please*?

England gave football to the world
Who, now they've got the knack
Play it better than we do
And won't let us have it back.

*Gareth Owen*

# Cross Porpoises

The porpoises
were looking really cross
so I went over
and talked at them

Soon they cheered up
and swam away
leaving laughter-bubbles
in their wake

It never fails,
talking at cross porpoises.

Roger McGough

# Sharp Freckles
## (for Ben Simmons)

He picks me up, his big thumbs under my armpits tickle,
then puts me down. On his belt there is a shining silver
        buckle.
I hold his hand and see, close up, the dark hairs on his
        knuckles.

He sings to me. His voice is loud and funny and I giggle.
Now we will eat. I listen to my breakfast as it crackles.
He nods and smiles. His eyes are birds in little nests of
        wrinkles.

We kick a ball, red and white, between us. When he
        tackles
I'm on the ground, breathing a world of grass. It prickles.
He bends. He lifts me high above his head. Frightened, I
        wriggle.

Face to his face, I watch the sweat above each caterpillar-
        eyebrow trickle.
He rubs his nose on mine, once, twice, three times, and
        we both chuckle.
He hasn't shaved today. He kisses me. He has sharp
        freckles.

*Carol Ann Duffy*

# Dracula

After we'd climbed the many roads from Efori Nord
by bus past Bucharest, the capital of Romania,
I was dog-tired. We went to a mountain room of pine,

and I searched the cupboards before I fell asleep.
That night I heard this weird flapping
at the window and woke up scared to death.

There, on the verandah, was a figure in black.
Casting no shadow. My hand instinctively flew
to my neck. Count Dracula was born here.

The cotton sheets were soaking with my sweat.
I could see his eyes flashing as he bent down;
imagine two small sinister holes in my skin.

If only we had stayed in Efori Nord,
playing ping-pong till Kingdom come.
If only we hadn't come to the mountains.

I crawled along the pine floor to my father's bed.
It was empty. Just a white pillow and a headrest.
My dad gave a loud guffaw from the balcony.

Took off his black cape; threw back his head,
said, 'Got you going there, didn't I?
Okay. The joke's over. Back to your bed.'

Can you believe that? All I am asking is:
who needs an imagination, a fear, or a dread,
when what we've got is parents instead?

*Jan Dean*

# Mr McGuire

Old Mr McGuire, blind as a bat,
had a rabbit, a weasel, a dog and a cat.
He stroked them all as he sat by the fire,
some days they felt smooth,
and some days like wire.
With a bark, a hiss, a squeak and miaow
they demanded attention
and all got it somehow.
Old Mr McGuire, he loved them all –
'To me you're one creature
you're all from the same sack.
God brought you here
and he'll take you back.
You may think you're all different
but, heavens above –
you are all of you loved
with one single love.'

Brian Patten

# The Owl and the Astronaut

The owl and the astronaut
Sailed through space
In their intergalactic ship
They kept hunger at bay
With three pills a day
And drank through a protein drip.
The owl dreamed of mince
And slices of quince
And remarked how life had gone flat;
'It may be all right
To fly faster than light
But I preferred the boat and the cat.'

# Friends

When first I went to school
I walked with Sally.
She carried my lunch pack,
Told me about a book she'd read
With a handsome hero
So I said,
'You be my best friend.'
After break I went right off her.
I can't say why
And anyway I met Joan
Who's pretty with dark curls
And we sat in a corner of the playground
And giggled about the boy who brought the milk.
Joan upset me at lunch,
I can't remember what she said actually,
But I was definitely upset
And took up with Hilary
Who's frightfully brilliant and everything
And showed me her history
Which I considered very decent.
The trouble with Hilary is
She has to let you know how clever she is
And I said,
'You're not the only one who's clever you know,'
And she went all quiet and funny
And hasn't spoken to me since.

Good riddance I say
And anyway Linda is much more my type of girl;
She does my hair in plaits
And says how pretty I look,
She really says what she thinks
And I appreciate that.
Nadine said she was common
When we saw her on the bus that time
Sitting with three boys from that other school,
And I had to agree
There was something in what she said.
There's a difference between friendliness
And being cheap
And I thought it my duty
To tell her what I thought.
Well she laughed right in my face
And then pretended I wasn't there
So I went right off her.
If there's one thing I can't stand
It's being ignored and laughed at.
Nadine understood what I meant,
Understood right away
And that's jolly nice in a friend.
I must tell you one thing about her,
She's rather a snob.
I get the feeling
She looks down on me
And she'll never come to my house
Though I've asked her thousands of times.

I thought it best to have it out with her
And she went off in a huff
Which rather proved my point
And I considered myself well rid.

At the moment
I walk home on my own
But I'm keeping my eyes open
And when I see somebody I consider suitable
I'll befriend her.

*Gareth Owen*

# 'The Fight of the Year'

'And there goes the bell for the third month
and Winter comes out of its corner looking groggy
Spring leads with a left to the head
followed by a sharp right to the body

> *daffodils*
> *primroses*
> *crocuses*
> *snowdrops*
> *lilacs*
> *violets*
> *pussywillow*

Winter can't take much more punishment
and Spring shows no signs of tiring

> *tadpoles*
> *squirrels*
> *baalambs*
> *badgers*
> *bunny rabbits*
> *mad march hares*
> *horses and hounds*

Spring is merciless
Winter won't go the full twelve rounds

> *bobtail clouds*
> *scallywaggy winds*
> *the sun*
> *a pavement artist*
> *in every town*

A left to the chin
and Winter's down!
     *tomatoes*
     *radish*
     *cucumber*
     *onions*
     *beetroot*
     *celery*
     *and any*
     *amount*
     *of lettuce*
     *for dinner*
Winter's out for the count
Spring is the winner!'

Roger McGough

# Leon Peabody Told Me a Secret

How secret's a secret? I want to know.
The one I've been keeping I have to let go.
It's making me burst, it's such a strain
Having a big secret locked up in my brain.
How secret's a secret? How long must it stay
Hidden inside me, bubbling away?

My tongue's in a knot, my jaws really ache,
It's late in the night but I'm wide awake.
Is there a limit on how long they last?
If so let me know when the limit has passed!
Secrets are time bombs, they can't help but blow.
If you have one keep silent – I don't want to know!

*Brian Patten*

# Mr and Mrs Lilac

Never go to the Lilacs' house
to fetch back your ball.
The Lilacs don't like children.
They don't like children at all.

Mr and Mrs Lilac steal children's balls.
They've got my balls, they've got my pals'.
Mr Lilac loathes you ringing his bell.
He says, 'It's my ball now, my ball.'

Mr Lilac smiles a terrible smile.
He watches you shake and tremble.
Mrs Lilac says, 'It's our land dear.
Our land. You should be careful.'

Once I peeped through their window.
The moon shone on my shadow.
Inside the Lilacs were playing ball.
There was haunting music in the hall.

An orange light glowed in the room.
Their faces were bright as broom.
Mr Lilac passed Mrs Lilac my basketball.
Mrs Lilac passed Mr Lilac Mugsy's rugby ball.

The strange thing was all our balls
looked new again, through the window.
Lisa's leather football, still bright white.
Django's tennis ball, feverish yellow tonight.

Nasreen's new golf balls, Jodie's bouncy balls,
Billy's baseballs, Pili's ping-pong balls.
I heard Mrs Lilac laugh through the window.
'Good throw, Mr Lilac, good throw.'

*Jan Dean*

# Spring Fashion Show

And now April saunters on
Looselimbed and goldenhaired
Wearing a see-through number
Of infinity-blue, appliquéd
With fluffy white clouds.

The designer gets a standing ovation.

(Same dress every year and we still fall for it.)

Roger McGough

# Prior Knowledge

Prior Knowledge was a strange boy.
He had sad green eyes.
He always seemed to know when I was telling lies.

We were friends for a summer.
Prior got out his knife
and mixed our bloods so we'd be brothers for life.

You'll be rich, he said, and famous;
but I must die.
Then brave, clever Prior began to cry.

He knew so much.
He knew the day before
I'd drop a jam jar full of frogspawn on the kitchen floor.

He knew there were wasps
in the gardening gloves.
He knew the name of the girl I'd grow up to love.

The day he died
he knew there would be
a wind shaking conkers from the horse chestnut tree;

and an aimless child
singing down Prior's street,
with bright red sandals on her skipping feet.

Carol Ann Duffy

# Naughty Nancy Noah

Three by three they came in,
All the clatter, all the din!
Two for the world when it was dry,
One to boil or bake or fry.
Mrs Noah had a cooking-pot
And she served up dinner piping-hot.

Three by three they came in,
Some were fat and some were thin.
The couples were easy but it was harder
Getting the rest into the larder.

'Hurry along! Walk! Don't fly!'
Said this evening's pigeon-pie.
'You hop first.' 'No, after you.'
Said tomorrow's rabbit-stew.

Three by three they came in,
All the clatter, all the din!
Two for the world when it was dry,
One to boil or bake or fry.
Mrs Noah had a cooking-pot
And she served up dinner piping-hot.

*Brian Patten*

# Den to Let

To let
One self-contained
Detached den.
Accommodation is compact
Measuring one yard square.
Ideal for two eight-year-olds
Plus one small dog
Or two cats
Or six gerbils.
Accommodation consists of:
One living-room
Which doubles as kitchen
Bedroom
Entrance-hall
Dining-room
Dungeon
Space capsule
Pirate boat
Covered wagon
Racing car
Palace
Aeroplane
Junk-room
And look-out post.
Property is southward facing
And can be found
Within a short walking distance
Of the back door
At bottom of garden.
Easily found in the dark

By following the smell
Of old cabbages and tea-bags.
Convenient escape routes
Past rubbish dump
To Seager's Lane
Through hole in hedge,
Or into next door's garden;
But beware of next door's rhinoceros
Who sometimes thinks he's a poodle.
Construction is of
Sound corrugated iron
And roof doubles as shower
During rainy weather.
Being partially underground,
Den makes
A particularly effective hiding place
When in a state of war
With older sisters
Brothers
Angry neighbours
Or when you simply want to be alone.
Some repair work needed
To north wall
Where Mr Spence's foot came through
When planting turnips last Thursday.
With den go all contents
Including:
One carpet – very smelly
One teapot – cracked
One woolly penguin – no beak and only one wing
One unopened tin
Of sultana pud

One hundred and three Beanos
Dated 1983-1985
And four Rupert annuals.
Rent is free
The only payment being
That the new occupant
Should care for the den
In the manner to which it has been accustomed
And on long Summer evenings
Heroic songs of days gone by
Should be loudly sung
So that the old and glory days
Will never be forgotten.

# Meeting Midnight

I met Midnight.
Her eyes were sparkling pavements after frost.
She wore a full-length, dark blue raincoat with a hood.
She winked. She smoked a small cheroot.

I followed her.
Her walk was more a shuffle, more a dance.
She took the path to the river, down she went.
On Midnight's scent,
I heard the twelve cool syllables, her name,
chime from the town.
When those bells stopped,

Midnight paused by the water's edge.
She waited there.
I saw a girl in purple on the bridge.
It was One O'Clock.
*Hurry*, Midnight said, *it's late, it's late*.
I saw them run together.
Midnight wept.
They kissed full on the lips
and then I slept.

The next day I bumped into Half-Past Four.
He was a bore.

Carol Ann Duffy

# The Poet's Garden

The garden is looking particularly all right at this time
of the year. There are yellow things everywhere and
sort of red bits in waving clumps. The lawn is as
green as grass and studded with
delicate little yellow and white
studs. Flowers, I think
they are called.

*Roger McGough*

# Mum Won't Let Me Keep a Rabbit

Mum won't let me keep a rabbit,
She won't let me keep a bat,
She won't let me keep a porcupine
Or a water-rat.

I can't keep pigeons
And I can't keep snails,
I can't keep kangaroos
Or wallabies with nails.

She won't let me keep a rattle-snake
Or viper in the house,
She won't let me keep a mamba
Or its meal, a mouse.

She won't let me keep a wombat
And it isn't very clear
Why I can't keep iguanas,
Jelly-fish or deer.

I can't keep a cockroach
Or a bumble-bee,
I can't keep an earwig,
A maggot or a flea.

I can't keep a wildebeest
And it's just my luck
I can't keep a mallard,
A dabchick or a duck.

She won't let me keep piranhas,
Toads or even frogs,
She won't let me keep an octopus
Or muddy water-hogs.

So out in the garden I kept a pet ant
And up in the attic !TNAHPELE TERCES A

# Word of a Lie

I am the fastest runner in my school and that's
NO WORD OF A LIE
I've got gold fillings in my teeth and that's
NO WORD OF A LIE
In my garden, I've got my own big bull and that's
NO WORD OF A LIE
I'm brilliant at giving my enemies grief and that's
NO WORD OF A LIE
I can multiply three billion and twenty-seven by nine billion
       four thousand and one in two seconds and that's
NO WORD OF A LIE
I can calculate the distance between planets before you've
       had toast and that's
NO WORD OF A LIE
I can always tell when my best pals boast and that's
NO WORD OF A LIE
I'd been round the world twice before I was three and a
       quarter and that's
NO WORD OF A LIE
I am definitely my mother's favourite daughter and that's
NO WORD OF A LIE
I am brilliant at fake laughter. I go Ha aha Ha ha ha and
       that's
NO WORD OF A LIE
I can tell the weather from one look at the sky and that's
NO WORD OF A LIE
I can predict disasters, floods, earthquakes and
       murders and that's

NO WORD OF A LIE
I can always tell when other people lie and that's
NO WORD OF A LIE
I can even tell if someone is going to die and that's
NO WORD OF A LIE
I am the most popular girl in my entire school and that's
NO WORD OF A LIE
I know the golden rule, don't play the fool, don't boast, be
	shy and that's
NO WORD OF A LIE
I am sensitive, I listen, I have kind brown eyes and that's
NO WORD OF A LIE

You don't believe me do you?
ALL RIGHT, ALL RIGHT, ALL RIGHT
I am the biggest liar in my school and that's
NO WORD OF A LIE

*Jan Dean*

# Scatterbrain

Before he goes to bed at night
Scatterbrained Uncle Pat
Gives the clock a saucer of milk
And winds up the tabby cat.

# Valentine Poem

If I were a poet
I'd write poems for you.
If I were a musician,
Music too.
But as I'm only an average man
I give you my love
As best what I can.

If I were a sculptor
I'd sculpt you in stone.
An osteopath,
Work myself to the bone.
But as I'm just a man in the street
I give you my love,
Lay my heart at your feet
                    *(ugh!)*

If I were an orator
I'd make pretty speeches.
An oil tanker,
Break up on your beaches.
But as I'm just an ordinary Joe
I send you my love,
As best what I know.

*Roger McGough*

# The Piano

The piano eats with chop sticks,
cool minims,
diced demi-semiquavers.

When the lid goes down
the piano is inscrutable,
shining with health.

The piano stands politely
until the next meal, silent
for as long as it takes.

Carol Ann Duffy

# Eight Brand New Angels
## (a counting rhyme)

Ten creepy criminals trying to commit a crime.
One got caught and then there were nine.

Nine juicy children on a giant's dinner plate.
One got eaten up and then there were eight.

Eight brand new angels on their way to Heaven.
One fell back to earth and then there were seven.

Seven dare-devils crossing the River Styx.
One dived in and then there were six.

Six melancholic milliners admiring a beehive.
One put it on her head and then there were five.

Five young sons going off to war.
One got blown to bits and then there were four.

Four mischievous boys teasing a chimpanzee.
One teased a rattlesnake and then there were three.

Three trapeze artists learning something new.
One failed to grasp the bar and then there were two.

Two men called Icarus flying towards the sun.
One quickly melted and then there was one.

One counting rhyme going on and on and on.
Suddenly it ended.
And then there was none.

Brian Patten

# Friendship Poems

(i)       There's good mates and bad mates
               'Sorry to keep you waiting' mates
       Cheap skates and wet mates
               The ones you end up hating mates
       Hard mates and fighting mates
               Witty and exciting mates
       Mates you want to hug
               And mates you want to clout
       Ones that get you into trouble
               And the ones that get you out.


(ii)     Two's company
         One's lonely

(iii)    I'm a fish out of water
         I'm two left feet
         On my own and lonely
         I'm incomplete

         I'm boots without laces
         I'm jeans without the zip
         I'm lost, I'm a zombie
         I'm a dislocated hip.


(iv)     When you're young
         Love sometimes confuses
         It clouds the brain
         And blows the fuses
         How often during those tender years
         You just can't see the wood for the tears.

                                   Roger McGough

# This and That

Two cats together
In bee-heavy weather
After the August day
In smug contentment lay
By the garden shed
In the flower bed
Yawning out the hours
In the shade of the flowers
And passed the time away,
Between stretching and washing and sleeping,
Talking over the day.

'Climbed a tree.'
'Aaaah.'
'Terrorised sparrows.'
'Mmmmh.'
'Was chased.'
'Aaaah.'
'Fawned somewhat!'
'Mmmmh.'
'Washed, this and that,'
Said the first cat.

And they passed the time away
Between stretching and washing and sleeping
Talking over the day.

'Gazed out of parlour window.'
'Aaaah.'
'Pursued blue bottles.'
'Mmmmh.'
'Clawed curtains.'
'Aaaah.'
'Was cuffed.'
'Mmmmh.'
'Washed, this and that.'
Said the other cat.

And they passed the time away
Between stretching and washing and sleeping
Talking over the day.

'Scratched to be let in.'
'Aaaah.'
'Patrolled the house.'
'Mmmmh.'
'Scratched to go out.'
'Aaaah.'
'Was booted.'
'Mmmmh.'
'Washed, this and that.'
Said the first cat.

And they passed the time away
Between stretching and washing and sleeping
Talking over the day.

'Lapped cream elegantly.'
'Aaaah.'
'Disdained dinner.'
'Mmmmh,'
'Borrowed a little salmon.'
'Aaaah.'
'Was tormented.'
'Mmmmh.'
'Washed, this and that.'
Said the other cat.

And they passed the time away
Between stretching and washing and sleeping
Talking over the day.

'Chased a shadow or two.'
'Aaaah.'
'Met friends.'
'Mmmmh.'
'Sang a little.'
'Aaaah.'
'Avoided water.'
'Mmmmh.'
'Washed, this and that.'
Said the first cat.

And they passed the time away
Between stretching and washing and sleeping
Talking over the day.

*Gareth Owen*

# So Shy

He was so shy he was born with a caul,
sort of a shawl made from the membrane
of the womb.  He was tongue-tied;

so shy he kept a dummy in his mouth
for 2 years; then, when that went,
a thumb. He was wide-eyed, dumb; so shy

he would hide in the cupboard under the stairs
for hours, with a bear; hearing his name called
from the top to the bottom of the house, quiet

as a mouse; shy as the milk in a coconut,
shy as a slither of soap. When he got droooed,
he wore shy clothes – a balaclava, mitts.

He ate shy food – blancmange, long-lasting mints.
He drank shy drinks – juice from a cup
with a lid and a lip, sip by shy sip.

He was so shy he lived with a blush,
sort of a flush under the skin, like the light
behind curtains on windows when somebody's in.

Carol Ann Duffy

# The Teachercreature

We held a seance in the kitchen,
Me, Jenny and Jo.
We covered the table with an old stained cloth
And turned the lights down low.
We summoned up a poltergeist,
A witch and a wizard too,
We summoned up a goblin
And an imp or two.
We summoned up a vampire,
A werewolf and a ghoul,
We summoned up a banshee
With a fearful howl.
Our hair turned grey, our knees gave way,
We trembled and felt sweaty,
And then we went and summoned up
A zombie and a yeti.
We summoned up a spectre,
A phantom and a spook,
We summoned up things so bad
We were scared to look.
Then last of all we summoned up
The world's most frightful creature.
We dashed out of the room because
It was our old schoolteacher.

Brian Patten

# Sassenachs

Me and my best pal (well, she was
till a minute ago) are off to London.
First trip on an intercity alone.
When we got on we were the same
kind of excited – jigging on our seats,
staring at everyone. But then,
I remembered I was to be sophisticated.
So when Jenny starts shouting,
'Look at that, the land's flat already'
when we are just outside Glasgow
(Motherwell actually) I feel myself flush.
Or even worse, 'Sassenach country.
Wey Hey Hey.' The tartan tammy
sitting proudly on top of her pony;
the tartan scarf swinging like a tail.
The nose pressed to the window.

'England's not so beautiful, is it?'
And we haven't even crossed the border.
The train's jazzy beat joins her:
Sassenachs sassenachs here we come.
Sassenachs sassenachs Rum Tum Tum
Sassenachs sassenachs how do you do.
Sassenachs sassenachs we'll get you.
Then she loses momentum, so out come
the egg mayonnaise sandwiches and
the big bottle of bru. 'Ma ma's done us proud,'
says Jenny, digging in, munching loud.
The whole train is an egg and I'm inside it.
I try and remain calm; Jenny starts it again,
Sassenachs sassenachs Rum Tum Tum.

Finally, we get there: London, Euston;
and the very first person on the platform
gets asked – 'are you a genuine sassenach?'
I want to die, but instead I say, '*Jenny*.'
He replies in that English way –
'I beg your pardon,' and Jenny screams
'Did you hear that Voice?'
And we both die laughing, clutching
our stomachs at Euston station.

*Jackie Kay*

# Mafia Cats

We're the Mafia cats
      Bugsy, Franco and Toni
We're crazy for pizza
      With hot pepperoni

We run all the rackets
      From gambling to vice
On St Valentine's Day
      We massacre mice

We always wear shades
      To show that we're meanies
Big hats and sharp suits
      And drive Lamborghinis

We're the Mafia cats
      Bugsy, Franco and Toni
Love Sicilian wine
      And cheese macaroni

But we have a secret
      (And if you dare tell
You'll end up with the kitten
      At the bottom of the well

Or covered in concrete
      And thrown into the deep
For this is one secret
      You really must keep).

We're the Cosa Nostra
      Run the scams and the fiddles
But at home we are
      Mopsy, Ginger and Tiddles.

(Breathe one word and you're cat-meat. OK?)

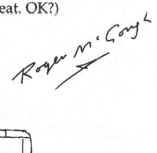

# Embryonic Mega-Stars

We can play reggae music, funk and skiffle too,
We prefer heavy metal but the classics sometimes do.
We're keen on Tamla-Motown, folk and soul,
But most of all, what we like
Is basic rock and roll.
We can play the monochord, the heptachord and flute,
We're OK on the saxophone and think the glockenspiel
        is cute,
We really love the tuba, the balalaika and guitar
And our duets on the clavichord are bound to take us far.
We think castanets are smashing, harmonicas are fun,
And with the ocarina have only just begun.
We've mastered synthesizers, bassoons and violins
As well as hurdy-gurdies, pan-pipes and mandolins.
The tom-tom and the tabor, the trumpet and the drum
We learnt to play in between the tintinnabulum.
We want to form a pop group
And will when we're eleven,
But at the moment Tracey's eight
And I am only seven.

Brian Patten

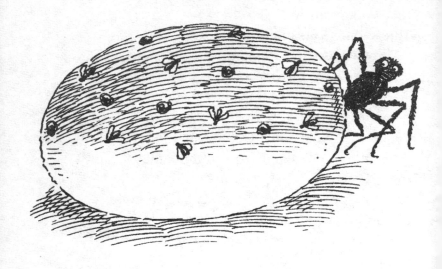

# Now the Spider's Web is Spun

on a currant bun
wise flies
hide in disguise

*Brian Patten*

# Three Young Rats

Three young rats in satin suits
  Three young cats in leather boots
    Three young ducks in gabardines
      Three young dogs in denim jeans
        Went out to walk with two young pigs
          In miniskirts and orange wigs
            But suddenly it chanced to rain
              And so they all went home again.

Roger McGough

# Sharon's Life

My name is Sharon
I have two brothers
Called Phillip and William
Sometimes they bother me
But often they don't.
Being me is fun.
When it is older
It won't be so good I think.
Phillip lost my book
It had pictures
He lost it
But I am not very cross.
Daddy bought it.
Aunt Judy died last week
Mummy said it was a loss
And then she cried
Quite a bit.
My dog is called Spot
He has some bad habits.
Perhaps I will find the book.
My bed is green.
I'm five.
That's all.
I'm glad I'm alive.

# Why Trees Have Got It All Wrong

Trees have got it all wrong
because they shed their leaves
as soon as it gets cold.

If they had any sense
they'd take them off in June
and let the scented breezes

whiffle through the branches
cooling the bare torso.
In high-summer, more so.

\*   \*   \*

Come autumn (not the fall)
they'd put on a new coat:
thick leaves, waxed and fur-lined

to keep them warm as toast,
whatever the weather.
Trees, get it together!

*Roger McGough*

# The Frog who Dreamed she was an Opera Singer

There once was a frog
who dreamed she was an opera singer.
She wished so hard she grew a long throat
and a beautiful polkadot green coat
and intense opera singer's eyes.
She even put on a little weight.
But she couldn't grow tall.
She just couldn't grow tall.
She leaped to the Queen Elizabeth Hall,
practising her sonata all the way.
Her voice was promising and lovely.
She couldn't wait to leapfrog onto the stage.
What a presence on the stage!
All the audience in the Queen Elizabeth Hall,
gasped to see one so small sing like that.
Her voice trembled and swelled
and filled with colour.
That frog was a green prima donna.

# Bouncing

Sally Arkari isn't she a treat
Bouncing her rubber ball
Up and down the street
Sticking-plaster spectacles
Braces on her teeth
Always scoffing chocolates
Always crunching sweets
Never stops bouncing
Wherever she goes
Never stops sniffing
Never blows her nose
She bounces when she's laughing
She bounces when she weeps
She bounces when she's wide awake
She bounces when she sleeps
She bounces in the playground
She bounces in the hall
You can always tell it's Sally
By her bouncing rubber ball
She bounces during Geography
She bounces during Art
She bounces all through dinner time
In the custard tart
She bounces till she's out of breath
And her face turns red
She bounces in assembly
On the teacher's head

She bounces to the fairground
And makes the people cross
As she bounces in the fish and chips
And in the candy floss
She bounces into Paris
And for almost an hour
She bounced her little rubber ball
On the Eiffel tower
She bounced down to the circus
And up the greasy pole
She bounced down to the football ground
And bounced into the goal
She bounced beside the brass band
As it marched around the town
She bounced among the drummer boys
And made them all fall down
She bounced it on her kneecaps
She bounced it on her head
Then she bounced her way back home again
And bounced into her bed.

Gareth Owen

# Chocs

Into the half-pound box of Moonlight
my small hand crept.
There was an electrifying rustle.
There was a dark and glamorous scent.
Into my open, moist mouth
the first Montelimar went.

Down in the crinkly second layer,
five finger-piglets snuffled
among the Hazelnut Whirl,
the Caramel Square,
the Black Cherry and Almond Truffle.

Bliss.

I chomped. I gorged.
I stuffed my face,
till only the Coffee Cream
was left for the owner of the box –
tough luck, Anne Pope –
oh, and half an Orange Supreme.

*Carol Ann Duffy*

# Conversation Piece

Late again Blenkinsop?
What's the excuse this time?
*Not my fault sir.*
Whose fault is it then?
*Grandma's sir.*
Grandma's. What did she do?
*She died sir.*
Died?
*She's seriously dead all right sir.*
That makes four grandmothers this term
And all on P.E. days Blenkinsop.
*I know. It's very upsetting sir.*
How many grandmothers have you got Blenkinsop?
*Grandmothers sir? None sir.*
None?
*All dead sir.*
And what about yesterday Blenkinsop?
*What about yesterday sir?*
You missed maths.
*That was the dentist sir.*
The dentist died?
*No sir. My teeth sir.*
You missed the test Blenkinsop.
*I'd been looking forward to it too sir.*
Right, line up for P.E.
*Can't sir.*

No such word as can't. Why can't you?
*No kit sir.*
Where is it?
*Home sir.*
What's it doing at home?
*Not ironed sir.*
Couldn't you iron it?
*Can't do it sir.*
Why not?
*My hand sir.*
Who usually does it?
*Grandma sir.*
Why couldn't she do it?
*Dead sir.*

*Gareth Owen*

# Born to Bugle

He was born to bugle
To be a bugler-boy
Not a teddy bear or a bouncy ball
But a bugle his first toy

He bugled before breakfast
In the bathtub and in bed
And in between he practised
Bugling on his head

He bugled on his bicycle
He bugled on the bus
At the zoo played boogie-woogie
With a hip hippopotamus

He bugled in Bulgaria
Botswana and Bahrein
Stowed below in cargo
Blowing bugle on a plane

He was born to bugle
Be bugling still today
But a burglar burgled his bugle
and took his breath away

And though we mourn the bugle
We mourn the bugler most
As laid to rest we do our best
To whistle 'The Last Post'.

Roger McGough

# The Pensive Pencils

I'm not scared of ghosts or of rats
Or of creaking doors or mice or bats,
I'm not scared of shadows or of owls
Or of hoots or squeaks or terrible growls,
I'm not scared of noises in the hall
Or of the things that slither and creep and crawl.
I'm not scared of things that moan and groan,
And I don't mind being left on my own.
But it's nearly midnight and I fear
The things I'm scared of are quiet near.
It's horrible! It's terrible! I might seem a fool,
But I really can't stand being locked in school

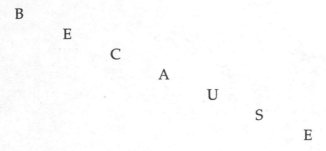

the Roundheads have come out of the history books,
There's a battle in the school hall,
There's a storm brewing up in the swimming-pool,
In fact it's become quite a squall.
The exercise books are puffing and panting,
They're doing press-ups in the gym,
The cat from the playground has joined them
In a feeble attempt to get slim.

There's a ghost of a cane in the cupboard,
The ex-pupils are rattling their bones,
The pens and the pencils are pensive,
And I'm locked in the school on my own!

Brian Patten

# At Home, Abroad

All summer
I dream of
places I've never
been
where I might
see faces
I've never seen,
like the dark
face of my
father in
Nigeria,
or the pale
face of my mother in
the Highlands,
or the bright
faces of my
cousins at
Land's End.

All summer
I spell the names
of tricky countries
just in case
I get a sudden
invite: Madagascar,
Cameroon. I draw
cartoons of
airports, big and small.

Who will meet me?
Will they
shake hands or
kiss both cheeks?
I draw
duty-frees
with every
country's favourite
sweetie, smiling
a sugary welcome,
and myself,
cap-peaked,
wondering if I am
'home'.

# The Going Pains

Before I could even understand
The meaning of the word 'command'
I've had them. The going pains.

*Go to your room*
*Go to bed*
*Go to sleep*

Twinges that warned of trouble in store
And once in the classroom, the more
I felt them. The going pains.

*Go to the back*
*Go and start again*
*Go to the Headmaster*

From year to year I hear it grow
The unrelenting list of GO.
That bossy word that rhymes with NO
Still can hurt. The going pains.

*Go*
*Go now*
*Why don't you just go.*

Roger McGough

# The Rival Arrives

Tom, take the baby out of the fridge
And put the milk back in.
We know you are not used to him
And think he makes a din,
But I'm afraid he's here to stay
And he is rather cute,
So you'll have to stop insisting
He goes in the car-boot.
And please stop telling all your friends
We bought him in a sale,
Or that he's a free sample
We received in the mail.
He was *not* found in a trolley
At the local Mothercare,
And a family did not give him to us
Because they'd one to spare.

You should look on the bright side, Tom.
In just a year or two
You will have someone else to blame
For the wicked things you do.

Brian Patten

# INDEX OF AUTHORS AND FIRST LINES

# CAROL ANN DUFFY

*Carol Ann Duffy*

Carol Ann was born in 1955 and read Philosophy at
Liverpool University. She has compiled anthologies for
young people including *Stopping for Death* which won
the Signal Award in 1996, and is currently writing a book
of poems for children. She lives in Manchester with her
daughter.

# JACKIE KAY

Jackie Kay was born and brought up in Scotland. She writes for adults and children. Her latest collection for children, *The Frog Who Dreamed she was an Opera Singer* is published by Bloomsbury. She lives in Manchester with her son.

# ROGER McGOUGH

*Roger McGough* [signature]

Having been born in Liverpool and played a minor, but heroic part in the Second World War, I emigrated to Canada and became a lumberjack before drifting south to herd cattle in Texas.

After a short spell as a rubber planter in the Amazon Rainforest, I returned to England in the hope of becoming rich and famous.

My hobbies are poetry and telling huge whopping fibs.

# GARETH OWEN

Gareth Owen was born in Lancashire of Welsh parents.
He was good at English and football but not much else.
His main ambition was to play inside forward for Everton.
He has been in the Merchant Navy, a market gardener, a
bookseller, a teacher and a drama lecturer. He writes novels,
poems and plays. His latest novel is *Rosie No Name and
the Forest of Forgetting*.

# BRIAN PATTEN

*Brian Patten [signature]*

Brian Patten was born in Liverpool. He has written poetry and plays for both adults and children, including the award-winning novel, *Mr Moon's Last Case*. His poetry collections for children include *Gargling with Jelly* and *Thawing Frozen Frogs*.

# ACKNOWLEDGEMENTS

The publishers would like to thank the following for
permission to reprint the selections in this book:

Carol Ann Duffy for 'Lies', 'So Shy', 'Prior Knowledge', 'Chocs', 'Sharp Freckles', 'Meeting
Midnight', 'Poker' and 'The Piano' © Carol Ann Duffy 1999.

Jackie Kay for 'The Frog who Dreamt she was an Opera Singer', 'Pomegranate', 'Mr and
Mrs Lilac', 'Word of a Lie', 'Summer Romance', and 'At Home, Abroad' from *The Frog
who Dreamt she was an Opera Singer* © Jackie Kay 1998 first published by Bloomsbury;
'Brendon Gallacher' and 'Sassenachs' from *Two's Company* © Jackie Kay 1992 first published by Blackie; 'Dracula' from *Three has Gone* © Jackie Kay first pubished by Backie.

Peters Fraser & Dunlop for 'Mafia Cats', 'Born to Bugle', 'Three Young Rats', 'Why Trees
Have Got It All Wrong' and 'The Going Pains' from *Bad Bad Cats* © Roger McGough 1997
first published by Viking; 'The Poet's Garden', 'Friendship Poems' and 'Valentine Poem'
from *Sky in the Pie* © Roger McGough 1983 first published by Kestrel Books; 'Spring
Fashion Show' from *Nailing the Shadow* © Roger McGough 1987 first published by Viking
Kestrel; 'Cross Porpoises', 'Bun Fight', 'Sloppy Ticks' and 'The Kleptomaniac' from *Pillow
Talk* © Roger McGough 1990 first published by Viking; 'The Fight of the Year' from *You
Tell Me* © Roger McGough first published by Kestrel books.

Rogers Coleridge and White Ltd for 'The Owl and the Astronaut' and 'Bouncing' from
*Song of the City* © Gareth Owen 1985 first published by Collins Children's Books;
'Sharon's Life', 'This and That', 'Our School', 'Friends', 'Den to Let' and 'Conversation
Piece' from *Salford Road* © Gareth Owen 1971, 1974, 1976, 1979, 1988 first published by
Kestrel Books; 'Scatterbrain', 'Moon' and 'Life as a Sheep' from *My Granny Is A Sumo
Wrestler* © Gareth Owen 1994 first published by Collins Children's Books; 'Can We Have
Our Ball Back, *Please*?' from *The Fox on the Roundabout* © Gareth Owen 1995 first pub-
lished by Collins Children's Books.

Rogers Coleridge and White Ltd for 'Leon Peabody Told Me a Secret', 'Mr McGuire', 'A
Bird, Dropping', 'Playing the Baby' and 'The Bogeyman at Number Twelve' from *The
Utter Nutters* © Brian Patten 1994 first published by Viking; 'Mum Won't Let Me Keep a
Rabbit', 'The Pensive Pencils', 'Embryonic Mega-Stars' and 'Eight Brand New Angels'
from *Gargling with Jelly* © Brian Patten 1985 first
published by Viking; 'The Teachercreature', 'Now the Spider's Web is Spun',
'The Rival Arrives' and 'Naughty Nancy Noah' from *Thawing Frozen Frogs* © Brian Patten
1990 first published by Viking.